Holiday Stress Relief: 10 Quick
Mindfulness Practices

Refocus Collection

by Erin E. Gleason Alvarez

Self-published. First edition, 2025.

ISBN: 979-8-9937873-0-5

www.takechargenegotiations.com

Disclaimer:

The information contained in this book is not intended as, and shall not be understood or construed as, legal, medical, psychological, or any other professional advice. This book is for educational and informational purposes only. Readers' utilization of this book – including implementation of any suggestions set out herein – does not create an attorney-client, nor a professional-client relationship, between readers and the author. The author expressly recommends that you seek advice from an attorney, doctor, counselor, or other provider, should you require professional assistance. The author has not made any guarantees about the results of taking any action recommended herein.

For my guys, who make every season brighter.

Contents

Foreword

When we hear the word "holiday," we often picture year-end celebrations. The truth is, holidays take many forms: family weddings, milestone birthdays, cultural or religious traditions, festivities, even reunions. Each event carries a mixture of joy, expectation, and excitement. Yet those feelings can also tangle with worries that everything will go exactly right, everyone will get along, and that you can afford the costs. The list of concerns often seems endless.

It is completely normal to feel both uplifted and stressed during these times. Since holidays are meant to be joyful, it can feel disheartening when stress, over-thinking, guilt, or exhaustion crowd out happiness.

I created this book to guide you through those moments when you want to look forward to a celebration, yet heavy feelings make it harder. Within these pages, you will find simple ways to reset your personal barometer so you can return to balance during your holiday.

In the following pages, you will discover:

How to set boundaries at family dinners (so political debates do not foreclose the possibility of dessert).

How to give gifts without guilt — even if resources feel stretched.

How to savor the moment, instead of trying to make the moment perfect.

How to manage work deadlines while preparing for a big occasion.

Personally speaking, holidays often arrived for me with the pressure to please everybody, to buy the best gifts in massive quantities, and to look ecstatic even when I was not feeling joyful. Over time, I learned to pause, reset, and find my way back to what mattered most.

This book offers you the same gentle reminders, so you can navigate holidays more calmly, with presence, and joy.

Chapter One

Set the Tone

Let us begin by considering how you want to feel as your holiday approaches.

This time, instead of starting with a to-do list, try something different. Step away from the fray for a moment. Close your eyes and think of the celebration ahead. Let go of what you think you should feel and focus on what feels genuine and best for you.

The goal of this exercise is to find new ways to enjoy your holidays that are authentic and fulfilling for you. We are often told that holidays are necessarily joyous, picture-perfect, harmonious. However, that may not suit you. Instead, you feel unhurried, grounded, or simply at ease.

Start with what feels true to you right now, not with what you think others expect of you. From that small, honest place, your season can begin to take shape in a way that is focused on choices that are yours.

Ask yourself:
"How do I want to feel during this celebration?"

Do not rush to find the perfect words or create a lengthy list of emotions. Simply breathe. After a few steady breaths, ask again: "How do I want to feel during this celebration?" See what arises naturally and write it down.

Perhaps as you breathe, certain words begin to surface — calm, balanced, curious, peaceful. Focus on what you want to experience, not what you hope to avoid. Anchored in positive intentions, you will begin to orient yourself toward a healthier, more grounded experience

If you find yourself stuck, visualize your ideal event. For instance, if it is your child's wedding, imagine the day unfolding with ease — the weather is gentle, the family getting along, your child radiant and loved. In that moment, what do you feel? Joy, hope, love, nostalgia, gratitude?

Notice how this mindset differs from one centered on avoidance. Thinking, "I just need to get through this wedding without losing it," only increases the pressure. Focus instead on what you want to feel (steady, joyful, connected) in order to expand your capacity to actually experience those emotions.

If your upcoming holiday is the long season that begins with Thanksgiving and carries you through to the New Year, ideally, this time is about connection, reflection, and gratitude.

Yet in reality, it can bring family tension, overindulgence, and exhaustion. Take comfort in knowing that you are not alone. The good news is that making the conscious decision to set your emotional thermostat can change everything. Yes, you can decide how you want to feel and let that be your experience.

Once you have identified two or three emotions you would like to embrace this season, create a small daily ritual to keep them close. A few quiet breaths in the morning, a note in your journal, a brief reflection before bed. Commit to a daily action that you enjoy, reminding you: this is how I am showing up for this holiday.

Turn the page for simple morning rituals to help you stay grounded and steady.

Chapter Two

Morning Reset

The days leading up to and throughout the holidays often evoke a range of emotions. Some of us may bounce out of bed with excitement, thinking of the fun that lies ahead. Some of us start the day feeling overwhelmed and tired. Others wish they could hide and ignore the entire experience because they feel sad or lonely during certain celebrations.

Many factors are outside of our control when it comes to holidays. Some holidays are simply etched into national or familial calendars. Others may be "by invitation." Regardless of the venue, you may not have any choice in the matter.

Whatever your experience, there are some things that remain under your control during holidays; this includes the decision as to whether you will respond or react to situations as they arise. Responding means you pause long enough to choose your words. Reacting means your emotions choose your response for you. Response comes from awareness; reaction comes from impulse. The pause between them is where presence lives.

To encourage more presence in your days, start slowly. Give yourself a few extra minutes every morning to do something that brings you back to the optimal emotions you wish to identify with for this holiday.

Meditation is a popular idea for this time. This can be an intimidating idea… sitting upright without thinking or itching your nose for a prolonged period. Ugh. However, it really doesn't need to be that intimidating or complicated. For years, doctors, mental health experts, and scientists have studied the benefits of regular meditation practice. The last word in that sentence is the key: it is practice. You commit to showing up every morning to spend some time with yourself - quiet, undisturbed time during which you agree with yourself to leave the to-do list behind and simply breathe.

Here is a simple way to do this:

You can begin by taking a few moments after you wake to contemplate one thing you are grateful for. Once identified, reflect on why you are grateful for this. Then, take a moment to gently breathe while counting your breaths. For example, take a deep breath (count one), then slowly exhale (count two). Count to ten, then start your day.

If you are still struggling with the thought of meditating all by yourself every day, you can download a meditation app. There are numerous free meditations that focus on various techniques, including breathing, visualization, and kindness practices. If one of those apps appeals to you, try something you are comfortable with that will restore your core emotions. Other options include journaling, listening to music that connects you to your holiday emotions, dancing to that music(!), or singing it out loud. You can also try a simple stretching routine or yoga that feels good for your body. Or go for a run or a walk, making sure to consciously connect with the emotions you value during this holiday.

Chapter Three

Arriving Before You Arrive

Before you enter a family dinner, a crowded party, or other holiday gathering, pause for a moment. Take a slow breath before you go in. Remember that this is your chance to arrive on your own terms, instead of succumbing to old habits or others' expectations. A brief pause helps you leave the hurry behind and choose a calm, centered entrance.

For example, we rarely arrive at a family holiday gathering with a clean slate. Instead, it is natural to carry our stories with us - it may be the last work email that came in… or we are preoccupied with the conversation from years ago that still makes us queasy, or even the worry we cannot quite put a name on.

Taking a moment for yourself before you enter the event restores your sovereignty; you reclaim control over your presence before external energy takes over. Sometimes, walking into a room full of people feels exciting. At other times, it affects your nerves, causes pressure, or stirs up long-buried emotions. You may feel there are unspoken expectations or old memories waiting to resurface. Either way, your energy matters.

Before you reach for the doorknob that leads to your festivities, slow down. Inhale gently, feeling your breath travel from your lungs into your belly, then exhale as slowly as you can. Let the breath steady you. Remind yourself that you can meet what is ahead with curiosity instead of caution, openness instead of armor.

Here, your breathing does not need to follow any particular technique; it is more about what feels good for you at that moment. By focusing on your breath, your attention shifts from worry to the present moment. You stop rehearsing small talk or contemplating the seating chart. You are simply breathing, and that small act softens your whole body. The moment becomes less about what others might think or do, and more about how you want to show up.

If the thought of walking into that space makes your stomach turn, that is OK. A short pause at the doorway will not change who is waiting on the other side, but it can change how you respond when you meet them. That breath is your quiet boundary, a signal to yourself that you choose calm over reaction.

If it helps, move a little more slowly than you usually do. Straighten your posture if that feels comfortable. Let your senses greet the space before your words. Pay attention to the scent in the air, the light, the sounds, the familiar faces, and the unfamiliar ones. Take in what is there, the atmosphere, without rushing into it. Notice one small detail that grounds you: a smell, the sound of music, a face that makes you smile. Let that be your connection.

Now, step through the doorway. You have already begun to change the room just by entering with your calm, authentic self.

Chapter Four

Boundaries

During the holidays, many of us feel compelled to make the people we love happy. It comes from a good place — the desire to care, to connect, to create moments that feel joyful. However, without boundaries, even kindness can drain you. When you keep saying yes while your body and mind are asking for rest, frustration builds quietly underneath the surface.

Saying no can be harder than one would assume. For many of us, it bumps up against who we have always been. You are the one who makes things happen — the host, the planner, the person who fills the gaps. You do it because you care, and because it is what everyone expects. But when you always step in, people stop noticing how much you are carrying. Before you know it, the same cycle repeats itself: you keep saying yes, everyone else relaxes, and you end up exhausted by the celebration you helped create.

Yet, boundaries are not walls. They are edges that define where your energy begins and ends. They help you to give from a place of choice, not obligation. Setting boundaries is not rejection — it is a sign of respect, for yourself and for others. When you honor your limits, you give others permission to do the same. You model what a healthy perspective looks like.

Saying "no" does not have to be harsh. A gentle "I wish I could, but I can't this time" or "I'm not in a position to help right now" is enough. You do not owe a long explanation or apology. What you owe, most of all, is honesty — to yourself and to the people you care about. Because when resentment starts to build, it does far more damage than a clear "no" ever could.

Remember, self-preservation is not selfish. Boundaries protect your energy so that what you do feels genuine and warm. When you say no to what depletes you, you make room to say yes to what nourishes you.

When the pressure starts to mount, stop and ask yourself: Am I saying yes because I want to pitch in? Or is it because I know something is expected of me?

If the answer is the latter, feel free to rethink it. Recall the emotions you have committed to feeling this holiday… that is where you want to stay grounded; those emotions set your baseline. And in all likelihood, you cannot get there if you say yes to

everything. Choose the yes that feels
right.

Chapter Five

Giving Without Guilt

Gift-giving is about connection; it is not a contest. Yet for many of us, giving gifts to the people we care about can start to feel like a performance measured in receipts and wrapping paper. We compare, calculate, and worry about how our gifts will measure up.

Giving is not meant to be a scorecard. It is simply a way to say, I see you and I care about you.

Somehow, gift-giving comes with pressure. Pressure to keep up or make up for some perceived shortcoming. When this pressure surfaces, however, remember that guilt and generosity do not mix well. Your loved ones do not want you to give out of obligation. It is time to release those feelings.

Think back on the holidays of your life. Which memories endure? Not the sweater that did not fit or the gadget that broke by February. What lingers are the small, human moments, the late-night laughter, the scent of something baking, the quiet gratitude of being together. Those moments are the true exchange.

Commercial culture urges us to buy more, give more, be more. It whispers that love requires proof. Yet love does not need evidence; it needs attention. When you give thoughtfully—for instance, something handmade, something chosen with care, or even something intangible like time—you restore the meaning that consumerism often buries. A simple card written with sincerity can outlast a gift that costs ten times the price.

This year, before you start shopping or scrolling, pause. Ask yourself: Why am I giving? To express appreciation? To ease guilt? To fill silence? Listen to that answer. If you choose to give, do it with an intention that feels good for you. Buy what aligns with your values and your budget.

If you decide not to give a physical gift, know that your time, kindness, or attention can mean more than anything in a box. Call a friend you have not spoken to in months. Send a card. Cook something you love and share it. Presence, given freely, nourishes connection far longer than objects do.

Release the guilt that says you must give to be loved. The truth is simpler: you are loved already.

In the end, presence always outweighs presents.

Chapter Six

When Joy Feels Far Away

Throughout this book so far, we have looked at ways of managing the stress, busy-ness, and aggravation that often accompany holidays. However, there is another side to holiday seasons, one that is not frantic or noisy, but one that is too quiet and sometimes very lonely.

While it is natural to feel frazzled before holiday dinners with family, it is also common to experience a pull at the heartstrings when the folks you used to sit down with are no longer there. Whether you have loved ones who have passed on or otherwise disappeared from your life, celebrating holidays without them can feel, plainly, wrong, displaced, sad, or as if it would be better to just forget the whole thing.

This chapter offers gentle ways to honor those feelings instead of pushing them aside.

When sadness overcomes the joy of the holiday season, making happiness feel like a distant memory, turn to mindfulness practices for support. For example, when you notice that pit in your stomach when you hear holiday music, take a moment for a small break. Take a deep breath in through your nose, hold it for a couple of seconds, then slowly release that breath. Do this a few times. If it is comfortable for you and you are in a safe space, close your eyes while you do this breathing exercise. Once finished, open your eyes if they were closed and focus on one thing that you see that brings you comfort If at home, it might be a book you loved reading, a candle that smells nice, artwork on your wall that you love. If you are out and about, notice the color of the sky, a scent in the air, the sound of birds talking to each other.

The world is bigger than one holiday event confined to a finite period of time. During that time, you have the choice to celebrate or not, but make that choice from a place of peace, rather than fear, sadness, or loneliness.

In the days or weeks leading up to the event, create small moments of self-care and comfort. You may want to designate a specific time every day for this — an hour, early in the morning, a midday break, or a nightly routine before bed — to help calm yourself down. Create a playlist of comforting music and listen to it often. Cook or bake something that you love (or buy it from somebody else if you do not want to cook). Spend time outdoors taking in fresh air, reading a book, or watching a movie that makes you laugh.

Before the holiday arrives, plan to avoid distractions and honor the self-care steps and desired emotions that you have identified. Would volunteering at a food pantry feed your soul? Perhaps going for a long run or bike ride would release the tension. Getting outside and going for a hike might offer a fresh perspective. How about hosting a small gathering of people you care about? What is an activity that you enjoy that will bring you back to yourself and provide some healing? Take the time to plan the details and make your celebration truly meaningful to you.

Mindfulness and celebration do not demand happiness. During holidays, these are tools that can help you stay open enough to notice how to access the peace and warmth within you.

Chapter Seven

Be Present, Not Perfect

What is the ideal, perfect holiday? Think about it. At the end of the day, what is the most important way for you to define your celebration? Is it photographing picture-perfect decor that is ready to upload to social media? Do you envision happy gatherings with family and friends, free from squabbles? Do you want to give and receive lavish gifts that are out of this world?

There is nothing wrong with wanting a beautiful experience until the pressures of maintaining that image outweigh the happiness it is supposed to produce. When you are scrolling Instagram, watching TV commercials, or the Hallmark channel, it is easy to believe that you are surrounded by happy, perfect holidays.

However, that is not reality, nor should it be. We are human, and the human experience is not a perfect one — but that is a good thing! What boring ingrates we would be if everything were perfect!

So, for your next holiday, start thinking of presence over perfection. Shift your outlook from perfecting every detail to simply observing what's right in front of you.

Being present can take many forms. It depends on what feels right for you. For example, being present might mean committing to being grateful for the little things all around you (the smell of food you love, a flicker of candlelight, the sound of rain falling outside your home). Embrace these sensory moments in order to deepen your appreciation of what already surrounds you.

Cultivate a heightened presence of your environment by committing to softer expectations when things go sideways. What if the cookies burned, Aunt Matilda brought green Jello mold to vegan dinner, or your child's diaper exploded all over their new picture-perfect outfit? Instead of treating these mishaps as a five-alarm fire, see them for the small, silly disruptions they are, and laugh. After all, aren't those the moments that become the best stories?

When you catch yourself worrying that the holiday you are planning is not good enough, simply observe that thought before it spirals. This is your opportunity to pause, take a break, reset, and return to what really matters to you.

Turn to the list of emotions that you created in Chapter One, representing how you want to feel this season. Now, turn those feelings into a phrase that you can repeat internally to remind yourself of what is really important right now.

For example, instead of saying to yourself, "It's not enough," think, "I feel grateful and excited for this holiday." This is a way of expressing self-compassion, while recognizing that imperfection does not mean failure. Focus on a statement affirming your values. Consequently, you will replace the negative feedback loop with a calmer, more compassionate mindset.

What do you want to remember about this holiday? A flawless presentation or the feeling of being truly aware and present? A perfectly polished holiday is fine for a TV commercial or a Reel, however, that's not real true life.

Thank goodness that we are not living in a commercial. Joy often lies in those moments that unfold unexpectedly.

Chapter Eight

*Closing the Laptop:
Managing Work Before You
Rest*

It feels overwhelming when deadlines collide with life stress before any big event (finishing work before a wedding trip, wrapping a pile of gifts before a birthday party). Instead of feeling the excitement build up, you may feel trapped at your desk, fearing that your workload will follow you throughout your holiday. Deadlines often masquerade as emergencies; what they really signify is a fear of disappointing others, losing control, or falling behind.

Mounting pre-holiday work stress can manifest in the way you interact with others in the workplace, your attention to detail in your work, how you relate to people you care about outside of work, and your ability to finally close your laptop for good once the holiday arrives. When deadlines take control of our work lives, it becomes easy to forget that time is one of our most precious and limited resources, and we must actively manage it in healthy ways.

As a starting point for managing your emotions during this time, set an intention for your relationship to your work during the upcoming holiday. Some people love their work, derive positive energy from it, and do not want or need a break during the holiday. On the other hand, others crawl towards a holiday, exhausted by work and counting the moments until they escape from it. Create a mindfulness practice in keeping with your holiday work intention (and the emotions you chose to honor during this period, from Chapter One). Here are some ideas to support you.

When the pressure builds, speed becomes our default mode.

Mindfulness asks for one breath before your reaction. If, in your attempts to finish work before your holiday, if you find yourself firing off emails at all hours, with less reflection and more haste, commit to pausing before you hit "send." Close your eyes, take a deep breath in, slowly release that breath. Then, open your eyes and read the email once more. Remember, you are not reading for grammar. Check your tone and the intention behind your message. Does the message provide clarity? Does it match the energy you want to bring to the relationship with the email recipient? Take a break to reflect on the messages you send, particularly when you are feeling stressed. These guiding principles can help prevent misunderstandings and regret.

Another stressor during holiday time is an overflowing calendar. Deadlines tend to multiply quietly. A calendar pause brings them into the light. We only have so many hours in the week, yet in the months and weeks leading up to holidays, our time can evaporate if we let it. On a weekly basis, check in with your calendar to observe where you have committed your time, and to evaluate whether that is what you genuinely want. Highlight those activities that align with your values. For those events that are misaligned: what can you eliminate or postpone? Are these commitments performative, or are they in sync with your values? Can you limit your participation in the obligatory events, opting instead for those you specifically choose?

Lastly, if you have decided to close up shop during the holiday, create a *hard stop* for yourself in advance. Set a clear, non-negotiable boundary around your work during this break. Ensure this boundary is clear with your coworkers and family. If you need a full rest from work, make sure your end date is clearly articulated before that time arrives. Then, stick to it. If you set parameters for work during a holiday, ensure that these are clear (for example, I will be available for email and phone calls from 7:30 to 8:30 AM EST on Tuesdays and Thursdays during the holiday).

As you leave for a holiday, find a symbolic act to help you transition from work to rest mode. Before you log off, take a moment to reflect on all that you have accomplished. Make a list of your priorities upon your return. Perhaps write a brief note to your future self, committing to starting work calmly when you return. Remember that rest is not something we earn by experiencing exhaustion; we must invite rest purposefully when we make a conscious commitment to it.

Chapter Nine

You Have Permission to
Leave the Table

Why is it that gatherings of people who care for each other so often devolve into arguments, passive-aggressive dealings, or broken relationships? Unfortunately, there is no clear answer. Perhaps old grievances have a way of resurfacing when the gang gets back together. Or the overconsumption of food or alcohol negatively impacts how people communicate with each other. Holding different political views from friends and family can also contribute to animosity around the holiday table.

Whether you are seated at Thanksgiving dinner or on a vacation cruise, when a disagreement crops up, it can feel uncomfortable for everybody. The energy of the festivities diminishes, people raise their voices in anger, instead of celebration. Suddenly, a happy occasion has turned toxic.

In these situations, one of the biggest problems is that people do not listen to one another. When Uncle Phil starts speaking, you tune out because you already know the political diatribes he is going to spew. Or when a parent remarks on your single status/choice of work/child with a stained shirt, you can immediately feel those walls building around you from defensive instincts.

Here are a few suggestions for navigating holiday drama without getting caught up in it. Before you approach the event, promise yourself that you will do so with curiosity, rather than expecting this year to be a repeat of past dramas. Give Uncle Phil a break, even if you do not really feel like he deserves it. You are giving him a break for yourself, not anyone else. Remember that you do not walk around with Uncle Phil all day. You may not understand what his life experience is, or what has informed his opinions. Use a holiday gathering as an opportunity to learn more about the people surrounding you, instead of hosting a festival of judgments about them in your head.

Once you arrive at the gathering, if the debate/argument/passive-aggressive discussion is launched, pause before you say anything. Remember that every moment does not need words. If you want to participate in the discussion, you don't need to chime in immediately. Instead, intentionally pause, breathe, and then consider what you want to say. Silence is not weakness - a moment of calm can outweigh even the loudest retort.

As the holiday unfolds, a commitment to curiosity. Initially, instead of adding your opinion or thoughts to the conversation, ask a genuine question. You may not like the answer, but at that point, you contributed to the discussion in a positive way. Sometimes, a well-paced question is enough to shift the tone.

If the conversation becomes toxic, remember that you do not have to match that energy. You have permission to leave the table. Go to the bathroom. Get something from your car. Visit the kitchen for a glass of water or step outside to get some fresh air. Taking a pause is not your helpless surrender; it is your valid interest in self-preservation. After you return, participate if it feels right.

Better conversations come from these small shifts. This holiday, protect your peace. Choose to communicate with others in an open, curious, and respectful way; when that is not possible, give yourself permission to quietly walk away. Leaving the table is not giving up; it's a strategic move. It is choosing calm over chaos — and that is always a win.

Chapter Ten

Quiet Holiday

There are years when the best way to celebrate is softly. And there are years when a quiet holiday arrives uninvited. Whether you are alone due to circumstances or choice, you can cultivate a restorative experience, one that is centered on renewal and reconnection, not isolation.

Sparkle and bustle are fine if you are in the mood for it. Sometimes, we simply need stillness and solitude. If you yearn for a holiday that is focused on replenishment instead of revelry, listen to that instinct. A quiet and personal retreat can be just as fulfilling (or more so!) than lively gatherings that demand your energy.

When you are celebrating solo by choice, remember: just as you have permission to leave the table, you have permission to leave the holiday and do your own thing. It is natural to feel that others might perceive your choice as selfish, antisocial, or against tradition. If you have had a tradition of celebrating with family and friends in the past, they may push back on your decision or express dismay about it. If your gut is telling you to stay home, you do not need to people-please and ignore your own needs. In this case, other people's reactions are usually based on their own discomfort with stillness, change, or even a perceived lack of control over the celebration. Nevertheless, this moment is about you, not them. Claim your quiet holiday without apology: "I'm looking forward to seeing you, just not on the day itself," or "I am keeping things simple this year."

If you are celebrating on your own due to circumstance, not choice, it is natural to experience sadness, longing, or confusion about what to do with the day. The sudden absence of other people, the noise of the holiday, or even the old routines of it might hurt. Rather than fighting those feelings or trying to suppress them, look to mindfulness for support. Return to the emotions you decided on in Chapter One to guide your holiday experience. Express how you are feeling in your journal, to someone you trust, or to a therapist. Look for ways to deepen your experience of your chosen holiday emotions by engaging in self-care activities that you enjoy (get a massage, jump on your bike, try a new hobby). As discussed in Chapter Five, plan the day well in advance. Start a new custom, honor a long-standing tradition that still brings you joy, or spend some time volunteering to help those in need.

In either circumstance, you may wish to make the choice to redefine what celebration means for you. Reflect on how a quieter, inner celebration can nourish your soul this holiday.

Holiday Mindfulness Companion

A gentle guide to help you put these practices into motion.

The *Holiday Mindfulness Companion* is designed to help you bring the ideas in this book into your everyday life, one step at a time.

In the following pages, you'll find 10 prompts inspired by the chapters of this book. Think of this as a way to invite a little mindfulness into your daily life, helping you pause, reflect, and reconnect when the holidays start to feel heavy and hurried.

Here are tips for using this section:

- Take a few minutes every day (or as often as you can) to focus on one prompt.
- After reading the prompt, sit with it for a moment.
- Next, use the blank space that follows, or your own journal, to jot down a few

words, thoughts, or
observations.

- Return to these pages
throughout the weeks leading
up to your holiday. Do your
answers change as the
holiday unfolds?

- Approach the exercise with
an open mind. No need to
resist or judge. Just be with
yourself.

Day 1: Set the Tone

Choose how you want to feel this week — calm, connected, light, or grateful.

Ask: What emotions do I want to guide my choices this season?

Day 2: The Morning Reset

Before checking your phone or starting your day, take a moment to breathe.

Reflection: What does "centered" feel like in my body today?

Day 3: The Doorway Pause

Before entering a room or engaging in a conversation, pause and take a moment to notice your breath.

Ask: What energy am I bringing with me?

Day 4: Boundaries with Grace

Say "no" kindly but clearly today - even to something small.

Reflection: *What boundary helps me stay grounded?*

Day 5: Releasing Judgment

Notice one moment when you catch yourself judging another person, a situation, or yourself.

Ask: What else might be true?

Day 6: Listening Over Speaking

Let one conversation today be about truly hearing.

Reflection: Did my curiosity change the tone between us?

Day 7: Midweek Check-In

Pause and scan your body — where are you holding tension?

Ritual: Stretch, breathe, or take a short walk in silence. Reset your pace.

Day 8: Choosing Positivity

Name three small things that went right today.

Reflection: Gratitude doesn't erase stress
— it shifts perspective.

Day 9: Quiet Evening Reset

Dim the lights early, slow your breathing, and let stillness return.

Ask: What does rest look like right now — not ideally, but realistically?

Day 10: Gratitude and Release

Acknowledge what this reset gave you.

Reflection: What will I carry forward into
tomorrow? What can I leave behind?

Acknowledgements

I am deeply grateful to my friends, family, students, clients, and colleagues who have shared their struggles and insights with me over the years. Your experiences (and mine) shaped every practice in this book.

To you, the reader who picked up this book... may you find the peace and presence you're seeking.

About the Author

Erin E. Gleason Alvarez is a law professor and professional mediator who has spent decades advancing conflict resolution, mindfulness, and the practical tools that help people navigate life's most difficult moments. She teaches law and mediation, specializing in negotiation, communication strategies, and how to stay grounded when emotions run high.

Her approach combines her professional expertise in conflict resolution with accessible mindfulness practices. As a mediator, Erin has helped countless individuals and organizations navigate high-stakes disputes, and she brings those same evidence-based techniques to everyday conflict management.

Continue Your Journey

Leave a review: If this book resonated with you, please share your thoughts where you purchased it. Your review helps others find these practices when they need them.

Coming soon: More books in The Refocus Collection are on the way, bringing practical mindfulness to life's most challenging moments.

Thank you for reading.

~ Erin